Dilemmas in Modern Science

Food
Ethical Debates on What We Eat

BY JIM KERR

A^+
Smart Apple Media

Contents

Introduction

Humans are pushing the boundaries of science and technology. We can access information at the touch of a button. We can genetically modify food so it grows faster and tastes better. We have developed medicines that can cure once fatal illnesses. All this might sound positive, but we are now facing many dilemmas in the areas of science, technology, and medicine. Just because we *can* do something, does this mean we *should*?

Many of these debates are based on what is ethically or morally right—for humans, for animals, or for the environment. People often feel very strongly about such issues, whether they are governments, special interest groups, or individuals. It is important for everyone to understand what these ethical questions are and to consider the ways in which they might be solved. The choices we make about what we eat are not only affected by what we like and do not like. Availability, health considerations, religious beliefs, and personal feelings about how food is produced are some of the other factors that may affect diet.

The use of fossil fuels in farming is contributing to climate change. Farming methods are one of many areas of debate about how food is produced.

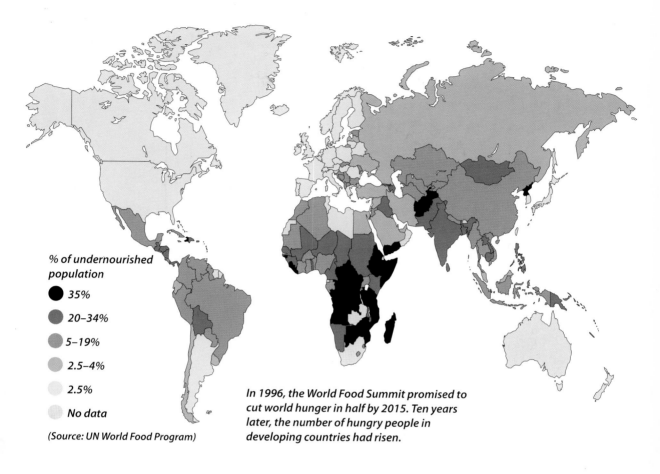

% of undernourished population

- 35%
- 20–34%
- 5–19%
- 2.5–4%
- 2.5%
- No data

(Source: UN World Food Program)

In 1996, the World Food Summit promised to cut world hunger in half by 2015. Ten years later, the number of hungry people in developing countries had risen.

Producers and Consumers

The production of food is the world's most important industry. Food provides energy for life. Farming businesses, agricultural machinery, chemical producers, plant-seed manufacturers, and food-processing companies all produce food. These large organizations, called "agribusinesses," have a great deal of power in deciding what we eat.

Governments can also affect the types of food produced, methods of production, and the way in which it is distributed. On a global level, environmentalists, food-safety advocates, and special interest groups for social justice have opinions on food. Nationally and locally, small independent farmers and informed consumers raise ethical debates about food. We all have a right and a duty to understand the views of these groups before we make our own decisions about what to eat.

Those Who Go Hungry

The United Nations Food and Agriculture Organization (FAO) estimates that 820 million people in less economically developed countries do not have enough to eat. But the world's population will grow from more than six and a half billion people today to nearly nine billion by 2050. Tackling hunger in the poorest parts of the world and producing enough to feed an even greater number of people in the future are two of the greatest challenges we face.

1 Where Does Food Come From?

Farming is the process of producing food by cultivating plants and raising domesticated animals. Early humans lived nomadic lives, moving from place to place. They gathered plants and other natural products from the land and hunted wild animals for food. About 10,000 years ago, people began to produce food by planting seeds in areas where the soil was rich, and there was a good supply of water for crops to grow. People settled in these farming regions, and communities began to grow.

Traditional Farming

Well into the nineteenth century, most farmers grew many types of crops and raised livestock. Sowing seeds, weeding, and harvesting were done by hand. Oxen or horses were used to pull basic farm machines such as plows. Soil was kept in good condition by crop rotation and the use of natural fertilizers. Farmers produced enough food to support their families, with perhaps a small surplus, which could be sold at a local market.

In some parts of the world, farming has not changed a great deal. In developing countries, small subsistence farms are run by single families. The soil is worked by hand to produce enough vegetables and fruit for the family to eat. Some animals may be kept to provide meat and milk.

In developing countries such as Nigeria, farming is still carried out in traditional ways. Planting is done by hand and the farmer produces just enough to feed his family.

The largest farms are areas of open grassland where cattle are raised. In the United States they are known as ranches. In Australia they are called cattle stations. These can be thousands of acres in size, with ranchers traveling across fields on horses or ATVs.

Farming Development

In many parts of Europe, North America, and Asia, a milder climate and richer soil provide more suitable farmland than the dry regions of Africa and the Middle East. The farming regions of more economically developed countries have had the most dramatic changes in food production. Developments in science, technology, and industry have been applied to agriculture, allowing larger areas of land to be farmed.

Intensive farming can be carried out on a huge scale. Often only a single crop is cultivated, all of which is sold. These farms are large businesses, producing vast quantities of food and generating a lot of wealth for the farm owner.

Feast and Famine

Large-scale farming that uses the latest technology produces greater yields. Food production using high-tech machinery also involves less labor. These factors reduce the cost of food production. The supporters of intensive farming—the agribusinesses—argue that bigger is better, because it produces large quantities of cheap food. But while wealthier nations create mountains of surplus food, hunger and famine are widespread in other parts of the world.

This is arguably the greatest ethical dilemma raised by food production. Should we expect the big businesses in the food industry to produce enough to feed the planet? Or can we now use technology to focus on improving farming conditions in the developing world, bringing water to dry regions, and making poor soil more fertile?

> **High-yield farming is the only way to save most of our wildlife, unless we are willing to destroy three billion living human beings.**
>
> *Dennis T. Avery*
> *Director, Center for Global Food Issues*

Today farming is a science. Research such as this, on crop plants in France, is carried out to find ways to improve the flavor, yield, and resistance to disease of different crops.

Technology and the Land

Powered machinery was first used in farming in the nineteenth century. Since this time, continuous developments in technology have provided increasingly efficient methods of crop production. Around the middle of the twentieth century, these developments brought about the "green revolution" in agriculture. Farming methods began to be influenced by agricultural scientists working in laboratories. These scientists developed chemicals to control pests and fertilize crops, and created new varieties of staple crops such as rice, wheat, and corn. Treated with the latest chemicals, these new species have resulted in much greater yields. The green revolution doubled food production between 1950 and 1980.

Today, agribusinesses use advanced technology to manage large farms. Computerized records provide information that influences decisions about the use of fertilizers and animal feed. Accurate weather forecasts are used in long-term planning. Technology has given farmers the tools to meet the increased demand for food from a growing global population.

YOU DECIDE

The introduction of new technologies means that fewer people are required to work in the agriculture industry than were needed in the past.

? *What effects might this have on people who rely on farming for their livelihood?*

? *Does the benefit of greater output outweigh the problem of unemployment?*

Dilemmas in High-Tech Farming

However, efficiency and greater yields come at a cost. Intensive farming relies on heavy industrial machinery that requires the use of large amounts of fossil fuels. Fossil fuels are a rapidly diminishing resource. At some point in the relatively near future, there may be none left. There is also evidence that the use of fossil fuels is contributing to climate change. Environmental groups such as Greenpeace believe these factors must be addressed when considering the long-term future of intensive farming.

Seeds, fertilizers, chemicals, and high-tech machinery are expensive, and in some cases only wealthy farmers can afford them. Technology has allowed wealthy farm owners to operate with a smaller workforce, increasing unemployment among farm workers. In this way, the green revolution has widened the gap between rich and poor in rural areas.

Small Farms

Not every farmer in the developed world uses modern technology and high-yield techniques. Traditional farming continues on some small farms. These farmers carry out mixed farming, in which a number of different crops and animals are raised, producing a small surplus, which can be sold. Some people believe these farms encourage biodiversity in rural areas. Small fields separated by fences or hedgerows and the growth of a variety of crops can help plants and animals survive in their natural habitats.

However, the output from these farms is small in comparison to that of large farms, and the farmers cannot sell their food at competitive prices. Do the benefits of large farms producing cheap quantities of a single crop outweigh the drawbacks of a less varied countryside that reduces the space for wild animals?

In traditional, small-scale agriculture, farmers grow small amounts of crops and raise livestock such as sheep and cattle. This type of farming is better for the environment than intensive farming, because it uses less fossil fuel and encourages biodiversity.

Wild Food

Since prehistoric times, humans have hunted wild animals and gathered wild plants. As agriculture and herding developed, food from domesticated crops and animals replaced wild food. More recently, the fish eaten by most people in developed countries has come from the nets of large factory-fishing ships. But hunting and gathering continue in many parts of the world and in many forms. These activities have given rise to several ethical questions—and a fierce debate about whether or not hunting and fishing should be permitted or banned.

Hunting and Fishing

The Inuit people of the frozen Arctic regions trap and hunt animals for food and clothing. Animal rights groups, such as People for the Ethical Treatment of Animals (PETA), believe it is unethical to treat animals as a resource in this way. The Inuit say it is part of their culture and way of life, and they should not have to change centuries of tradition.

In most cases, consumers have the option of buying fish caught in the wild, but overfishing has become a concern. Some experts, including the United Nations FAO, believe that many species will disappear from the sea within 50 years if fishing is not more carefully controlled.

It is now possible to grow species of popular fish, particularly salmon, in fish farms. However, this has raised new dilemmas. The chemicals used in salmon farming might cause pollution, and some studies suggest that farmed fish may be less healthy than fish caught in the wild.

Fishing regulations are used by government and environmental agencies to protect stocks of wild fish. Even anglers are restricted by these regulations.

GLOBAL LOSS OF SEAFOOD SPECIES

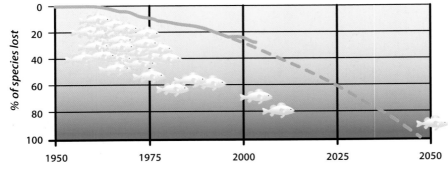

% of species lost

0 — 20 — 40 — 60 — 80 — 100

1950 1975 2000 2025 2050 *(Source: FAO)*

Experts believe that by 2050, species of fish currently being caught for food may disappear unless authorities introduce stricter limits on fishing.

Saving the Whale

By the late nineteenth century, the hunting of whales for oil and food had become such a huge industry that many species were in danger of disappearing from the oceans. To prevent this, international agreements have been put in place to protect the whale. By the mid-1980s, most countries had agreed to a ban on whaling, except when it is carried out for scientific research. However, some countries, including Norway and Japan, have refused to accept this agreement.

Opponents of whale hunting argue that it is wrong to hunt endangered species. They may also support animal rights, claiming that the killing methods are cruel and inhumane. Representatives of pro-whaling countries such as Japan point out that whales cannot be farmed like fish or livestock. They also say they are researching more humane ways of killing whales and are therefore addressing one of the main areas of concern. Some anti-whaling nations have been accused of ethical double standards, because they permit other forms of hunting. Does this inconsistency show a failure to recognize and respect different traditions?

YOU DECIDE

Many animal species have become endangered by being hunted and killed for food.

? *Is it right to introduce laws that prevent people from hunting animals if it has been part of their culture for centuries?*

? *Is tradition a good enough reason to continue hunting animals for food?*

? *Whose needs should come first, those of people or animals?*

Many people believe that hunting whales, an endangered species, is wrong and that the methods are inhumane. This Japanese whaling ship took three attempts to kill the whale.

2 Animal Welfare and the Environment

Animal welfare and the effects of certain farming methods on the environment are two of the most contentious issues in food production today. Animal rights activists and environmental groups undertake high-profile campaigns to prevent techniques introduced by governments or other agencies that activists believe are cruel or damaging. These groups encourage more humane and sustainable methods of food production.

Livestock Farming

The development of artificial fertilizers has made intensive crop farming possible, but it is not only fruit, vegetables, and grains that can be cultivated in this way. Large-scale animal farming is now possible through new methods of reducing and controlling the spread of disease. These allow livestock to be raised in confined spaces, protected from exposure to natural hazards. As with intensive crop farming, intensive livestock farming (also called factory farming) produces greater yields than other methods.

This calf is being given an injection of antibiotics. The development of such preventative medicines has made intensive farming possible. Animals can now be kept confined without fear of diseases being easily spread.

The Advantages of Intensive Farming

Intensive farming is widespread in developed countries, and most of the meat, dairy products, eggs, fruit, and vegetables sold in supermarkets are produced in this way. Agribusinesses and giant food companies say that large-scale intensive farming allows food to be produced at low cost. They argue that these savings are passed on to the consumer, making food more affordable, particularly for people with low incomes.

They also argue that intensive livestock farming is safe and efficient. Confined livestock can be supervised more closely than free-range animals, and diseases can be treated more quickly should they develop. Intensive farming has also been justified on the grounds that a more efficient production of meat, milk, or eggs requires fewer animals to be raised. This can limit the negative effects of agriculture on the environment.

The Disadvantages of Intensive Farming

Contrary to what agribusinesses claim, opponents say that intensive farming still causes environmental problems. Large quantities and concentrations of animal waste are produced. Disposal of this, unless carried out properly, carries the risk of pollution, particularly to fresh water supplies. Critics also point out that large numbers of animals require high volumes of fresh water, reducing supplies in some areas. However, the most common objection to intensive livestock farming is the way animals are treated.

INTENSIVE FARMING IN THE DEVELOPING WORLD

It has been suggested that intensive livestock farming methods should be introduced more widely in developing countries. Benefits such as higher yields and lower costs may help farmers in poorer communities. However, such farming would not offer employment to many local people and would use resources, such as water, which are scarce in many of these countries. It would also be costly to provide the facilities, and who should pay?

Hens raised for laying eggs are kept in rows of small cages. This is called battery farming.

YOU DECIDE

Many people think factory farming is cruel and unnecessary, but there are arguments in its favor.

? *Is factory farming acceptable if it brings down the cost of meat so that people in poorer communities can afford it?*

? *Traditional methods of farming were no less "cruel" than factory farming. Have we become too sentimental about animals?*

Questions of Cruelty

Some opponents of intensive farming object to it on the grounds that keeping animals in tightly packed pens or cages is inhumane. Groups such as PETA, the largest international animal-rights organization in the world, point to scientific research showing that hens and pigs kept in barren conditions suffer physical problems such as joint pain. Some animal scientists have shown that repetitive or self-destructive behavior is more common on factory farms than on farms where animals are free to move around. By publicizing these studies, activists have raised awareness of the conditions in which battery animals are kept, and there is a strong public following for campaigns against intensive livestock farming.

> 66 *Animals on factory farms gain weight, lay eggs, or produce milk, not because they are well cared for, comfortable, or content, but because their bodies have been manipulated with medications, hormones, genetics, and management techniques.* 99

PETA

PETA has publicized some of the more controversial aspects of factory farming relating to animal welfare. This demonstration took place in New Delhi, India, in 2006.

Some consumers are choosing to eat less meat, but they are willing to pay more for free-range and organic products as a reaction to intensive farming methods.

Health Issues

It is not only animal welfare and environmental issues that concern opponents. Recent food-safety concerns have focused further attention on this method of livestock farming and have suggested that despite the use of antibiotics, disease still spreads when animals are crowded together. It is now believed that intensively raised cattle host harmful bacteria such as E. coli that are resistant to antibiotics and the natural defenses that once protected humans from diseases naturally occurring among animals.

Food producers argue that by continuing to use intensively farmed animal products, they are simply meeting the demand for cheap meat and poultry. Many consumers are clearly unaware or unconcerned about the conditions in which animals are kept on factory farms. They place a great deal of trust in government food regulations that set health and safety standards in food production. Consumers may also believe that as long as food is cooked properly, the bacteria will be killed and the risk of disease removed. On the other hand, concerns about intensive animal farming have affected the retail sector, as some consumers have demanded products that are free range or grass fed. Many supermarkets now offer these alternatives, because shoppers are prepared to pay more for them.

BSE

In 1986, a major outbreak of BSE (bovine spongiform encephalopathy), or "mad cow disease," occurred in the United Kingdom (the UK). The use of animal byproduct feeds, including bone meal from sheep, had lowered the cost of intensive cattle farming. However, after cows became sick, tests showed that this had resulted in the spread of BSE to 178,000 animals. It is thought that eating beef from cows infected with BSE can cause CJD (Creutzfeldt-Jakob Disease) in humans, and a number of people died from the disease. Although it has now been controlled, the UK is still suffering the effects of the export bans that were put in place at the time. In 2003, the first cases of BSE were discovered in the U.S.

This farmer in Mississippi wears protective clothing while he sprays his crops with insecticides.

HERBICIDES

Herbicides are a short-term solution used to kill weeds. However, repeated use of herbicides—instead of plowing weeds under the ground—can disturb the tiny organisms that live in the soil. These help break down plant residues, which in turn rebuild nutrients in the soil. If this process is upset, soil can become less fertile over time.

Environmental Issues

Another of the key ethical debates in food farming relates to how modern methods are affecting the environment. It is not just the extensive use of depleting resources such as fossil fuels that is causing concern among environmental groups. Scientific and technological developments might offer faster, cheaper, and more effective alternatives to traditional farming, but intensive agriculture has a negative effect on the environment because it relies heavily on the use of chemicals.

Soil Erosion and Public Health

In intensive farming, fertilizers and plant-growth regulators assist crop growth. Artificial products such as insecticides and pesticides are also used to destroy weeds, fungi, and pests that attack crops. Chemicals are used in growth hormones for animal farming.

Environmental groups such as Friends of the Earth believe too many chemicals are used in intensive farming. They say it is contributing to pollution and harming natural resources, particularly soil. By using artificial fertilizers instead of replacing natural materials that help plants grow, intensive farming slowly breaks down soil structure. It becomes increasingly likely to suffer from erosion.

Many people are concerned about the chemical sprays used in intensive farming. The use of pesticides is particularly controversial. Some of the first chemical pesticides introduced were later found to be dangerous. The deadliest of these, such as DDT (dichloro-diphenyl-trichloroethane), have been banned in many countries. However, in some poorer parts of the world, cheap pesticides are still used.

The supporters of agribusinesses say that in most cases, pesticide levels in foods are within safe limits. But consumer groups, organic farmers, and health activists believe that the long-term health effects of mixtures of different pesticides are difficult to determine.

Water Pollution and Waste

Chemical fertilizers are rich in nitrates. If used in large quantities, nitrates can be washed away from farmland and into groundwater and rivers, making the water dangerous to drink. Applying science and technology to crop growth produces greater quantities of food, but is it worth the risks that chemical fertilizers carry into rivers and streams?

Intensive farming relies on large quantities of chemicals and fuel for farm machinery and creates a high volume of waste. But people who represent agribusinesses have argued that the negative claims of environmental groups are exaggerated or inaccurate. The arguments, claims, and counterclaims are extremely complex, just as they are in other areas of debate about what we eat.

When fertilizers get into water, they allow algae to grow more quickly than normal in a process called eutrophication. This pollutes the water, preventing the plants beneath the surface from getting enough sunlight to flourish.

3 New Foods

Biotechnology is technology based on the study of living things, especially when used in agriculture, food science, and medicine. One of the earliest forms of biotechnology was the use of tiny organisms to make organic products such as beer and cheese. Malted grains are combined with organisms called yeasts to produce beer. In cheese making, the process of fermentation is applied to dairy products. Although it has been used for centuries, modern developments in biotechnology have raised many ethical concerns.

Biotechnology is not a new idea. For many years, farmers have studied plant growth in order to select the best-suited and highest-yielding crops. They learned to "breed" one successful plant with another to improve and vary crops in a scientific process known as artificial selection. They would even crossbreed animals to improve the quality of their livestock. The huge advances in technology today are making it increasingly easy to modify food to the farmer's best advantage.

New Biotechnology

Biological science continues to be used in the production of food suitable for humans. The most recent use of biotechnology in agricultural

This scientist is grafting together two plants to see if the resulting new type of plant has a higher resistance to disease than the two original plants.

Animals can be modified by crossbreeding to produce stronger and healthier ones. This calf is a crossbreed.

science is in the field of genetic engineering. This produces varieties of plants that have yields and disease resistance far superior to those occurring naturally. Genetic engineering has opened up other fields of biotechnology. It can be used to modify plants, animals, and even humans. Although it offers a wealth of opportunity for greater yields and better products, many have questioned the ethics of interfering with nature in this way and have asked where we should draw the line in developing artificial breeds of living organisms.

> **Any effort to deny access to technologies that are demonstrably helpful in feeding the people of the world must … be judged from a moral and ethical point of view in relation to its real, not imagined, effects on human welfare.**

Peter H. Raven
Director of the Missouri Botanical Garden, in a speech given to the Vatican about modified organisms

YOU DECIDE

Many people assume that biotechnology cannot be misused. Therefore, they believe it is free from ethical dilemmas, but others argue it is not that simple.

? *Is it acceptable to alter the genetic structure of an organism just for profit?*

? *Is life, in all its forms, sacred, or is it acceptable to view certain organisms as commodities? Where do the boundaries lie?*

? *What ways might there be to limit the ethical concerns of biotechnology while still enjoying its benefits?*

What Are GM Foods?

Genes are the tiny parts of a plant, animal, or human that control all its characteristics. Genes dictate the color of our eyes or our hair, for example. Genetics is the scientific study of how genes pass features from one generation to another.

Some food available today may be the result of genetic modification (GM). This is a process by which the cells of an organism are altered. Two genes with desired characteristics are split and combined to produce a new gene. This is cut into a cell, which multiplies to form a new organism. Each of its cells contains the altered genetic information with the desired properties. Scientists first learned how to alter the genes of an organism in 1973, and GM foods have been available since the 1990s.

MODIFIED RICE

In March 2007, the United States Department of Agriculture (USDA) approved commercial production of a new variety of rice. This rice has been genetically modified with human genes. As a result, the rice will contain human milk proteins, which can be extracted and used for rehydration drinks. These will be used to treat illnesses such as diarrhea in children in the developing world.

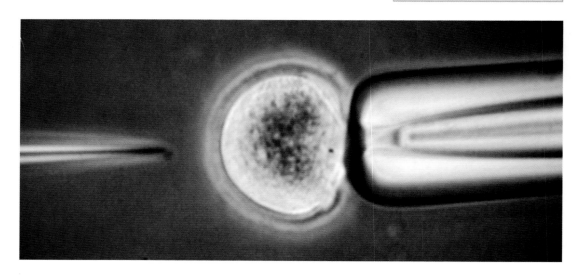

Types of Genetic Engineering

There are two types of genetic engineering: adding a gene from the same species or adding a gene from a different species. Through these methods, scientists create crops that will grow more quickly or in greater abundance. Researchers have also developed genes that make plants better able to survive drought. Once a new GM seed has been produced, scientists test the seed to make sure the gene transfer has been successful. Experiments on GM crops are carried out under real farm conditions to make sure they grow well, and GM foods are tested to make sure they are safe to eat.

To genetically modify an organism, genes are taken from one organism and injected into the cell of another. The genes are placed in the nucleus of the cell (the dark patch in the middle of the cell in the picture). Organisms can also be modified by removing genetic material in a similar way.

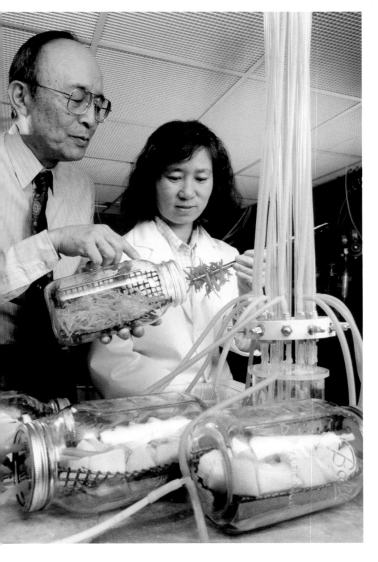

These scientists are conducting experiments on fruit to find ways of making it last longer once it has been harvested.

GM Produce

The most common GM crops are soy beans, corn, cotton, and rape seeds. Soy beans and rape are used to make oils and margarine. They are modified to resist certain herbicides, which means farmers can spray fields with weed killers without damaging the crops. Corn and cotton seeds have been modified to carry a poison that kills pests and protects crops against damage. GM crops are mainly grown in the U.S., Argentina, Canada, China, Brazil, and South Africa.

Despite the obvious benefits of GM foods, they have been surrounded by controversy since the first types, genetically modified tomatoes, became available in the U.S. In 1994, the U.S. Food and Drug Administration (FDA) announced that GM tomatoes were safe to eat and did not require special labeling. Since then, GM foods have become widely available in the U.S. However, they have only recently been accepted in many European countries, where they must be clearly labeled.

> **It is fairly certain that some GM foods will cause problems. Low risk is not no risk. The question is one which is universal in economics—will the benefits outweigh the costs?**

Steve Jones
Geneticist

Support for GM Food

By fundamentally changing the food we eat, GM has become a hugely controversial issue. GM food businesses say their products are the solution to feeding a growing population. Since GM crops are able to resist insects, disease, and spoilage, farmers can produce much higher yields and reduce waste. Greater and more reliable crop harvests will keep down the cost of food.

Supporters of GM production say it offers a better way of managing land than intensive farming. Disease-resistant species require fewer chemicals, so crop spraying can be reduced. They also say it is possible that GM seeds could be farmed in places where conventional crops have failed. This may help feed people in less fertile areas of the world.

The Risks of GM Food

So, if genetic modification can result in cheap, nutritious food in less fertile areas, what is the problem? Some people argue that GM foods are still very new. No major health hazards have come to light since GM food was introduced, but groups such as the Organic Consumers Association in the U.S. say it is too early to determine the long-term health risks.

Environmental groups claim we do not yet understand the impact of genetic engineering on plant or animal health. Some tests have already shown that GM crops are leaking toxins from their roots into the soil. This may affect soil fertility and produce new species of pests. Like some consumer groups, they also urge a more cautious approach to the development of GM food.

GM companies focus on profitable crops such as corn, cotton, and soy. Opponents say this is at the expense of new varieties of rice and cassava, which could be grown in the drier climates of the developing world. These people are farming GM soy in Romania.

At the moment, consumers can choose whether they wish to eat GM products or not. However, insects, birds, and wind could carry seeds and pollen from GM fields to other areas. If this occurs, GM plants may start to breed with organic plants. If that happens, people will not have a choice about what they eat.

Bio Power

One of the biggest issues to arise from the development of GM food is the motives of the biotech industry that researches and produces GM products. The seeds and weed killers with which GM crops must be sprayed are made by a handful of big companies. Anti-globalization activists say these companies will attempt to maximize the amount of money they make from their products. In traditional farming, farmers save seeds from a harvest to plant the following year. Biotech companies require the farmers who grow GM crops to buy new seeds every year, and this gives the seed companies great power, particularly over farmers. Is it right that big corporations have such control over what we eat and how it is produced?

YOU DECIDE

GM food is about bigger and better crops, but issues such as the power of large companies have caused many people to question GM ethics.

? *Do the benefits of higher volumes of GM products, especially the part this could play in tackling world hunger without requiring additional land, outweigh the uncertainties about GM food?*

? *Should profit be a driving force behind this kind of technology?*

Consumer groups and activists fear biotech companies may become so powerful they will be able to put pressure on food regulation bodies such as the FDA. The protestors pictured here are hanging onto the anchor of a ship transporting GM food, owned by the multinational company Monsanto.

Organic farming began with small, independent producers, but as demand for organic food increases, production is becoming large scale. This is a large organic farm in the UK. The rows of compost in the distance are composed of horse manure used as a natural fertilizer.

Organic Farming

Biotechnology is not the only area in which new foods have become available in recent years. As biotechnology developed, the organic movement began as a reaction to intensive farming and other modern techniques. This movement rejects many of the developments in agricultural science, for example, the use of chemicals to fertilize soil and control pests. Instead, traditional and natural methods such as crop rotation, manure, and compost, are used to increase soil health over time.

"100 Percent Organic"

Legislation and certification standards on organic foods were introduced in the 1990s. In the U.S. and most of Europe, organic farming is now clearly defined by law. Organic certification requires farms to meet certain standards. For example, land must be farmed organically for a period of time before produce can be labeled as organic. Methods of organic farming vary, but organic farmers share a number of basic aims. These include protection of the soil, promotion of biodiversity—for example, growing a variety of crops rather than a single crop—and outdoor grazing for livestock and poultry.

Since the early 1990s, organic farming has become increasingly widespread, and around two percent of farmland now is organic. A number of factors have

> **"** *Industrialized, chemical-intensive agriculture and our globalized system of distributing food and fiber are literally destroying the Earth, driving two billion farmers off the land and producing a product which is increasingly contaminated. That's why the wave of the future is organic and sustainable, not GMO.* **"**
>
> **Ronnie Cummins**
> *Organic Consumers Association*

These people are trying organic food at a farmers market. Many people claim that organic food tastes better and is healthier.

increased demand for organic products. These include concerns about conditions in factory farms and health scares following specific events, such as the BSE outbreak in the UK. Recent concerns about GM food have also encouraged some people to "go organic."

The Natural Cost

The arguments for and against organic farming tend to involve consumer and environmental groups on one side and agribusinesses on the other. Those who support this method of food production say it creates more jobs in rural communities, because it requires more human labor than farming which uses a lot of machinery. They also believe that naturally produced food is healthier and better for you than food cultivated using chemicals.

Agribusinesses counter these arguments, pointing out that organic farming is less productive. If everyone returned to traditional methods, there would not be enough food for the growing population. They also argue that because it is more labor intensive, it is more expensive, and these high production costs are passed on to consumers in urban areas.

Although there are valid arguments against widespread organic farming, ethical issues such as sustainability and support for small producers have contributed to its successful growth. As the movement continues to grow and more and more people start buying organic food, demand will increase. At some point in the future, supply may not be able to keep up with this demand.

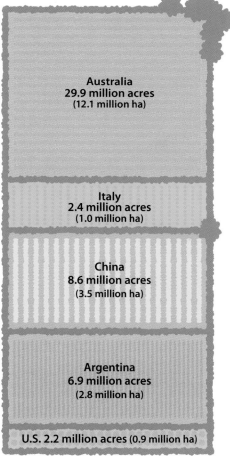

Australia
29.9 million acres
(12.1 million ha)

Italy
2.4 million acres
(1.0 million ha)

China
8.6 million acres
(3.5 million ha)

Argentina
6.9 million acres
(2.8 million ha)

U.S. 2.2 million acres (0.9 million ha)

This chart shows the five countries with the largest areas of organic farmland. Globally, there are around 76 million acres (31 million ha) of organic land contained within these five countries.
(Source: The World of Organic Agriculture 2007)

4 Food Distribution and Marketing

The green revolution and intensive farming have dramatically increased food production in some parts of the world, and several developed nations now produce much more food than they need to feed local populations. However, other areas have not yet benefited from new farming technologies. In some places the land is not fertile enough to farm, or the machinery, fertilizers, and other chemicals are too expensive for farmers to buy. So while some countries produce too much food, farming methods in other countries make the food too expensive for local people to buy. The ethical questions relating to this dilemma include if and how food should be more evenly distributed.

Waste Not, Want Not?

In richer countries, many farmers receive government support in the form of subsidies. They may be paid to produce as much as possible of certain crops. Overproduction may provide food to spare for years when harvests are poor, and the excess can be sold to other countries, which creates wealth.

Thousands of tons of fresh produce are destroyed in developed countries. Because the amount of food available affects its price, in some cases food is destroyed to keep prices high.

In some cases, vast surpluses of food are produced. Overproduction would seem to be a good thing. It is surely better to have too much than not enough. The food can be sold cheaply to developing countries, where people might be more in need of it. This can have a negative effect on local suppliers who are forced to lower their prices in order to compete. In addition, some poorer countries cannot afford the cost of transportation needed to distribute the food to people in need, who might live in remote rural areas.

Some foods that are overproduced can be put into storage. However, fresh fruit, vegetables, and meat cannot be stored or sent quickly enough to areas suffering from food shortages.

Meat production requires intensive land use. This land could be used for cultivating crops that could be stored longer and distributed more easily to parts of the world where they are needed.

Unequal Shares

Each person needs an average of 2,400 calories each day to stay healthy. Most people in the developed world, where there is plenty of food, receive much more than this. In fact, many people consume too much sugar, fat, salt, and animal products. This can cause illness, particularly obesity.

At the same time, many people in the developing world eat less than they need to stay healthy, often because they cannot afford to buy locally produced food. The problem of world hunger is not that we do not produce enough food to feed everyone. The issue is that not enough food reaches the people who need it most, because they cannot afford it.

❝ *Almost every location on Earth can produce enough food for its population. Even Bangladesh is self-sufficient in food production. The challenge is that people cannot earn enough to buy the food that is available.* ❞

The Hunger Project

Tackling Hunger

Many parts of the developing world have experienced famine, when a country or region does not produce enough food to feed its people. Famine can be caused by natural disasters such as floods, earthquakes, and crop failures, or by wars that create food shortages.

One possible solution to ending hunger is to use intensive farming methods and GM crops to increase the amount of food produced in developing countries, making the best use of the available farmland. Critics of this solution say intensive farming will destroy land in the long term, making infertile regions even more dependent on the developed world.

New varieties of native cereal crops that grow in hot climates have been discovered in Africa. These could be farmed in ways that keep land fertile for the future. Some people also believe that organic farming will help conserve farmland and create jobs in the developing world. However, this will require more land to be used.

Cash-Crop Farming

In some parts of the developing world, farmland is used to grow crops such as peanuts, coffee, tea, and cocoa. These are called "cash crops" because they are not used by local people. Instead, they are sold overseas to make money. The money is then used to buy essential food such as rice and corn. Although this can provide a solution to economic

Education is an important way to help farmers in the developing world. Here, an aid worker talks to farmers in Tanzania, Africa.

difficulties in these regions, some argue it would be better for poorer countries to use land to grow their own food rather than to raise it for export. Aid agencies and groups such as the Sustainable Agriculture Center for Research Extension and Development (SACRED) in Africa, believe the way to help small farmers in developing nations is to provide better education and technology. Giving money for farm equipment and tools helps farmers improve their land and make better use of it. It also encourages them to become self-sufficient and to work in ways that are sustainable (*see* page 32).

Food aid may be in the form of loans that allow developing countries to buy food, or packages that are airlifted directly to problem areas. Here, U.S. aid parcels are collected for distribution in Afghanistan.

Food Aid

Countries that produce an excess of food can help regions that have suffered food shortages by providing food aid. This can be carried out by governments or charities such as Oxfam, which raise money through donations.

Food aid is a good way to help regions where hunger and famine have been caused by a sudden emergency. However, aid agencies such as ActionAid say the long-term goal must be to resolve the problem of underproduction. They also point out that finding a better way of sharing the world's food is needed in order to address the problem of hunger.

FAIR TRADE

The food companies that sell fair-trade goods are trying to help developing nations overcome underproduction. The small farmers who produce many fair-trade goods receive a greater share of the profits from the sale of these products. Fair-trade companies try to work with suppliers who operate plantations on which workers are treated fairly. More than one billion dollars were spent on fair-trade goods worldwide in 2005.

The volume sold in 2005 (in tons) of six of the most common fair-trade products. (Source: FLO International)

Coffee 37,458
Tea 2,881
Rice 1,877
Sugar 3,981
Cocoa 6,234
Bananas 114,472

Sustainable Development

One of the main ways of ensuring a more even distribution of food crops and addressing the food shortages in poorer nations is to develop sustainable methods of agriculture. But sustainable development will not only benefit developing countries. There are productivity issues all over the world. The green revolution increased farm productivity up to about 1980, but some studies suggest that food production has now begun to fall. It is possible that soil is being damaged by overuse, heavy use of chemical fertilizers, and bad drainage of water.

Experts say that even developed countries must switch to methods of farming that are more sustainable. They argue that scientific research, careful land management, and conservation of resources must all be considered

by farmers and food producers. As part of this sustainable development, we must look at ways in which fuel and water can be used more efficiently, as these are dwindling resources.

This scientist is conducting an experiment to find ways of reducing soil erosion by covering the soil with straw. Such experiments may be essential to the long-term future of sustainable agriculture.

The Cost of Sustainability

Support for sustainable farming raises difficult ethical questions. People in the developed world have grown used to having an abundance of cheap food, but some say that we can no longer make decisions that are based on short-term

MONOCULTURE

Monoculture is the practice of growing one crop at a time in a particular field. It has been encouraged by the rise in intensive farming, farm subsidies in the developed world, and cash-crop production in the developing world. Some experts believe that monoculture is unsustainable, especially if the same crop is grown year after year. They say it is necessary to manage soil so that it remains productive in the long term. This means varying the type of crops grown so overused land can have an opportunity to recover.

> *The goal of sustainable development is to enable all people throughout the world to satisfy their basic needs and enjoy a better quality of life, without compromising the quality of life of future generations.*
>
> UK government, 2005

Land clearing is a particular problem in Brazil, where large areas of the rain forest are being cut down and burned to make way for cattle farming. The cattle are then allowed to overgraze, which causes soil erosion, leading to desertification.

benefit. The global population continues to grow and resources are becoming more limited. Environmentalists believe that we must consider the long-term ability of natural habitats to recover and regenerate.

Groups that support sustainable development, such as the international Alliance for Sustainability, are not against global economic growth. Instead, they seek to structure this growth in ways that will ensure long-term survival rather than short-term benefit. They also support the goals of relieving poverty, creating a more equal standard of living, addressing the problems caused by over- and underproduction, and satisfying the basic needs of all people. These goals are often not compatible with the

methods of big businesses. A key question is whether governments are willing to support sustainable development. There are encouraging signs. For example, farm subsidies are used in the U.S. and some European nations to encourage farmers to set aside fields for the benefit of land and wildlife.

Ultimately, the ethical dilemmas in food production and distribution encompass environmental issues, the demands of consumers in the developed world, the need to encourage global economic growth, and the basic human rights of farmers in developing nations. At the moment, sustainable development seems the best way of reconciling these issues so the largest number of people will benefit.

Supermarkets have great power over producers. Recently, they have begun to insist that fruit and vegetables are produced to a certain standard size.

How Food Is Sold

Science and technology have changed the way food is distributed. Today, refrigeration allows food to travel long distances from its source. In the developed world, supermarkets use vast and complex transportation, packaging, warehousing, and retail networks. They are able to meet the demand for a huge choice of cheap food that looks good on the shelves and is available all year round.

The role of supermarkets in the production and retailing of food has generated fierce debate and raises many ethical issues. The buying power of the largest companies allows them to put pressure on producers, increasing the problems in the developing world by pushing prices artificially low. Supermarket chains can still make profits on the food because they sell such large quantities.

FOOD MILES
The supply networks used by supermarkets lead to food being transported long distances before it is delivered to supermarket shelves. The distance food is transported is known as "food miles" and it impacts traffic levels, pollution, and fossil-fuel use. In North America, products clock an average of 1,500 food miles before appearing on supermarket shelves.

Global and Local Foods

Buying power and global distribution networks allow supermarkets, helped by free-trade agreements between countries, to source food from all over the world. Supermarkets say their customers want low prices. Large farms run by global agribusinesses are able to meet these demands, but small farmers need fair prices to stay in business. This is particularly true in developing countries, and has led to the growth of fair-trade products (*see* page 31).

In developing countries, the local market is the place to buy food fresh from the farm or sea. Farmers markets, in which producers sell directly to the public, have become increasingly popular in developed countries because people believe this method of selling is better for the environment than the global supply-chain used by supermarkets. Local produce does not travel as far, reducing food miles. The food also requires less packaging, which reduces the amount of materials needed.

Small Goods

The wholesale prices that farmers receive for their produce are very low, but farmers who sell directly to the public without going through a retailer get a better price. By shopping at farmers markets, consumers help small and sustainable farms stay in business.

Agribusinesses respond that buying locally produced goods may have a negative impact on developing countries, which rely on food exports. But supporters say that buying local food does not necessarily reject all food from overseas. They argue that it favors local in-season food, where this is available.

As consumers make ethical choices about food distribution and the environment, it is interesting to see that supermarkets have begun to offer more local products.

Fears about food safety have increased the desire to know exactly where food, especially meat, has come from. At farmers markets, shoppers can inspect the food and ask questions.

5 Food and Health

The changes in the ways that food is produced, distributed, and sold have raised many issues. But ethical questions about food go beyond concerns for animal welfare, damaging the environment, and the unequal balance of supply and demand in parts of the world. Once food reaches the consumer, the ethical dilemmas become very personal. They affect our health and our way of life. We all have to make decisions about how and what we choose to eat.

Many people in developed countries eat more food than they need. Some people argue that we should return to a diet that includes fewer meat products, which was more common 30 years ago. This might help address the problems of unequal distribution of food in the world.

The Obesity Epidemic

In developed countries, where there is an abundance of food, many people eat more than is good for them. Obesity is the condition of excess fat in the body. It is caused by weight gain resulting from individuals consuming more calories than they use. Obesity carries an increased risk of developing certain diseases. According to the World Health Organization (WHO), it is one of the greatest public-health challenges of the twenty-first century.

The Causes of Obesity

A number of factors have been identified as possible causes of obesity, including genetics. However, many experts agree that the most significant factors are lack of exercise and a diet high in sugary, fatty food.

Rates of obesity have risen significantly in many parts of the world during the past few decades. There are a number of possible reasons for this. Food production has increased, and the cost of many foodstuffs, particularly sugar, is much lower than it was in the past. Large amounts of cheap food are available, and this has encouraged people to consume it in greater quantities. Today, many individuals lead busy lives, which promotes unhealthy eating. People have come to rely increasingly on prepackaged fast food. Fast-food products are made with ingredients that maintain a certain flavor or consistency, preserve freshness, and are low cost. This is achieved by food engineering: the use of additives and processing techniques that alter the natural form of food. These methods of production generally reduce the nutritional value of the product.

Finding a Fat-Buster

The U.S. has the highest rate of obesity of any nation in the developed world. Considerable money is spent on drug treatments for obesity. A number of drugs can limit its effects, as can special surgical procedures. However, drug treatments carry the risks of side effects such as high blood pressure, and surgical procedures also carry risks. In addition, patients must make changes to their diet for the rest of their lives to keep the weight off. Some believe that drugs and surgery are quick fixes for a problem with multiple, complex causes. One ethical dilemma is that in group health plans, the cost of treating health problems related to obesity raises premiums for everyone. Should people take more responsibility to eat healthier foods and live a healthier lifestyle?

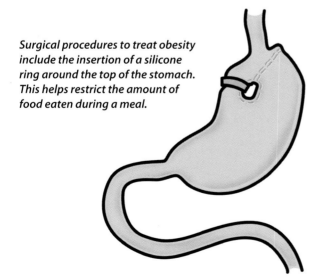

Surgical procedures to treat obesity include the insertion of a silicone ring around the top of the stomach. This helps restrict the amount of food eaten during a meal.

FAT FACTS

■ *The most common measure of obesity is Body Mass Index (BMI), in which a person's weight is considered relative to height. It can also be measured by waist circumference.*

■ *Obesity can lead to the following medical problems:*

Arthritis

Heart disease

Diabetes

■ *The U.S. has highest rates of obesity in the developed world. During the period from 1980 to 2002, obesity doubled in adults and tripled in children and adolescents.*

YOU DECIDE

Overeating and obesity are becoming increasingly widespread in many countries.

? *Should there be a total ban on advertising fast food?*

? *Is it acceptable to eat food that is bad for you, as long as it is done in moderation?*

? *Should people be dictated to about what they can and can't eat?*

Adding Value?

The inclusion of additives such as colorings, flavorings, artificial sweeteners, and preservatives in food products has raised other health concerns and ethical dilemmas. Special interest groups, for example, those concerned with hyperactivity and ADD in children, have campaigned against some products. They point to claims by experts that certain ingredients in sweets and carbonated drinks increase this type of behavior. It would seem obvious that artificial chemicals in foods are not good for health, and ethically there is no reason for them to be included since they are only there to make food look better, taste better, or last longer.

The companies that produce these foods, which could include anything from prepackaged microwave meals to candy, claim they are simply responding to consumer demands. They say that people would not buy food if it went bad after a few days or had natural coloring. In these cases, should there be stricter controls on what is included in our food, or should people be allowed to make their own decisions as long as they know the facts?

Researchers are finding ways of improving the nutritional value of certain foods by increasing mineral, vitamin, and protein content. Eliminating artificial additives is a big step toward addressing health issues.

In 2007, several species of seafood raised on farms like this in China were investigated by the FDA. They were found to contain drugs and additives that were not approved by the regulatory body.

Food Rules and Regulations

Making it clear what is contained in any food product is a big step toward giving people the information they need to make important personal decisions about what they choose to eat. Information such as the name of the product, a list of ingredients, a use-by date, and storage instructions have all appeared on food packaging for a number of years. More recently, however, stricter guidelines have been introduced by regulatory bodies such as the FDA in the U.S. and the Food Standards Agency in the UK. In most cases, food manufacturers are required to conform to strict, legal guidelines, and food safety and standards are carefully monitored.

Nutritional Information

Concerns about obesity and other issues have focused much attention on the importance of food labeling. Today, nutritional claims are tightly regulated. Manufacturers who say their products contain reduced fat or are rich in vitamins, for example, are now required to meet compulsory standards. The UK is considering "traffic light" labeling to indicate how healthy foods are. Regardless of their ethical position, the big food companies and supermarkets are required to follow any rules established by their country's regulatory body. However, although the ethical issues are being considered, they are not always being acted on.

Personal Choices

Personal decisions about how and what we eat are not only related to the content of food. They can also be dictated by individual moral, ethical, or religious beliefs. For example, people might choose to be vegetarian for health reasons, or they might not eat a certain type of food, such as pork, because it is forbidden by their religion. They may opt only to buy organic food because they believe it is better for the environment.

Vegetarians and Vegans

Vegetarianism is the practice of not eating meat. Some people also refuse to consume animal products such as dairy and eggs. This is veganism. Many vegetarians and vegans will not wear clothing or footwear that is made from skins, fur, or silk. Vegetarianism was practiced for religious reasons in Europe as early as the sixth century B.C. It continues to be observed for religious reasons in all parts of the world. Most Hindus, for example, are vegetarian. Some people follow a vegetarian diet for health reasons. They believe it has a better nutritional balance. Ethical choices are also a strong factor for many vegetarians. Some people believe it is wrong to slaughter animals, as well as raise animals in factory-farm conditions. Economic vegetarians have made choices about what they eat based on concerns about hunger in developing nations.

Most people live healthy lives as vegetarians. Some studies indicate that vegetarian diets may contain insufficient quantities of iron or calcium, but important vitamins and minerals can also be found in green leafy vegetables, grains, nuts, and fortified juices or soy milk.

Olympic champion Carl Lewis is vegetarian. Vegetarian diets are consistent with the Dietary Guidelines for Americans and can meet Recommended Dietary Allowances for nutrients.

RELIGIOUS GUIDELINES
Religious beliefs influence several dietary choices. Islam permits meat to be eaten only if it is halal, *or slaughtered according to Islamic standards. The Jewish religion places certain restrictions on meat, and eating meat and dairy products together is forbidden.*

Jewish food must be kosher, or prepared in a way that conforms to Jewish laws. For example, animals must be slaughtered in a way that minimizes their suffering.

Green Concerns

Many meat eaters are now choosing products that are organic or free range. Organic products are free from additives, pesticides, hormones, and other substances that cause increasing debate. A growing number of meat eaters are uncomfortable about the conditions in which poultry and cattle are raised.

Future Choices

In the past 100 years, developments in science and technology have allowed us to produce more food, but these developments have relied on the availability of fossil fuels and fertile farmland. Producing an increased amount of food will need to take into account the challenge of sustainability. We must all ensure that power sources and fertile soil continue to be available. The choices we make about food ultimately depend on its continuing availability.

Omega 3 is a useful supplement for vegetarians. It can be found in oily fish such as mackerel, as well as plant-based sources such as leafy, green vegetables.

YOU DECIDE

There are several organizations that encourage more widespread vegetarianism as a reaction to issues such as factory farming.

? *Where does encouragement end and unnecessary pressure begin?*

? *Should people be made more aware of where their food comes from, for example, by being made to visit a battery farm?*

? *Do people have the right to make a personal choice about what they eat without being made to feel guilty about it?*

Time Line

1850
The American Vegetarian Society is formed.

1929
Unilever, the first international food company, is established.

1930
Frozen food goes on sale in the U.S. for the first time.

1942
Organic Farming and Gardening is published in the U.S.

1945
The United Nations (UN) sets up the Food and Agriculture Organization to lead the fight against hunger in both developed and developing nations.

1948
The World Health Organization is established.

1955
The first McDonald's hamburger stand is set up in the U.S.

1979
The UN establishes October 16th as World Food Day in an effort to heighten awareness of food issues around the world.

1980
PETA (People for the Ethical Treatment of Animals) is formed in the United States. It grows to become the largest international animal rights organization in the world.

1985
The Live Aid concert is held to raise money for famine relief in Ethiopia. The Farm Aid concert is held to raise money for small family farms in the U.S.

1986
The Slow Food Movement begins in Italy, supporting the sale of local and organic food. The International Whaling Committee bans commercial whaling.

1991
The Nutrition Task Force is established in the UK to promote a greater understanding of health and nutritional issues across the country.

1994
The Flavr Savr genetically modified tomato is approved by the FDA and goes on sale in the U.S.

2001
An outbreak of foot-and-mouth disease in the UK leads to the slaughter of four million animals.

2004
The European Union lifts its ban on GM crops, but insists they must be clearly labeled.

2007
The USDA approves commercial growing of rice containing human genes, which will be used to treat illnesses such as diarrhea in the developing world.

More Information

● Books

Food (Planet under Pressure) by Paul Mason, Heinemann, 2006

Food and Farming (The Global Village) by John Baines, Smart Apple Media, 2009

Food and the World (Your Environment) by Julia Allen, Stargazer Books, 2007

Food for Life (Sustainable Futures) by John Baines, Smart Apple Media, 2007

Genetically Modified Food (Global Perspectives) by Vicky Franchino, Cherry Lake Publishers, 2008

World Hunger (At Issue) by Susan C. Hunnicutt, ed, Greenhaven Press, c2007

● Websites

www.who.int/en World Health Organization.

www.fda.gov U.S. Food and Drug Administration.

www.usda.gov U.S. Department of Agriculture website.

www.theglobaleducationproject.org/earth/food-and-soil.php Collection of broad-based factual information on the state of the world's environment.

www.organicconsumers.org Information of interest to organic consumers in the U.S.

www.vrg.org Information, advice and recipes for vegetarians.

www.kidsnutrition.org/consumer/archives/ Articles on topics ranging from healthy eating habits to nutrition for vegetarian teens.

www.slowfood.com Information about the Slow Food Movement, which encourages local and organic food traditions.

www.wpf.org World Population Foundation information on issues relating to the growth of the global population, including food.

www.peta.org People for the Ethical Treatment of Animals, the world's largest animal rights organization.

Glossary

additives artificial substances that are added to food for a specific purpose, such as to preserve or improve its flavor.

agribusiness a large-scale farming business.

antibiotics drugs such as penicillin that are used to treat infections and diseases.

artificial selection a method of breeding animals and plants to produce species with desirable characteristics.

bacteria tiny organisms that can cause disease.

biodiversity the variety of plant and animal species that exists within an environment.

biotech company a company that produces the seeds and treatments used in the production of genetically modified (GM) food.

cash crops crops that are grown specifically for direct sale or export.

certification a guarantee that required standards have been met. For example, foods must fulfill certain criteria and be certified before they can be labeled organic.

crop rotation a method of farming in which different crops are grown on the same piece of land each year in a repeating cycle.

cultivate to grow crops or plants.

developed countries the richer countries of the world, where large-scale industry takes place, creating jobs and wealth.

developing countries the poorer countries of the world, in which farming rather than industry is usually the main way of life.

erosion the process by which soil, rock, and other substances are worn away by wind or water.

factory fishing fishing in which large ships catch huge amounts of fish, processing and refrigerating them on board.

fair trade trade in which organizations negotiate a fair price with food producers to allow them decent working conditions, health care, and other basic needs, plus reinvestment to allow for a sustainable future.

fermentation the process by which an organic molecule is split into simpler substances.

fertilizers chemicals or natural products that are added to soil to encourage plant growth.

fossil fuels resources that come from the remains of plants and animals, formed over millions of years. Fossil fuels include coal, oil, and natural gas.

free-range relating to the system in which livestock is allowed to move about freely.

free trade a system in which goods and services can be bought and sold without being subject to government control.

genetic modification (GM) the process of making some food products bigger, better, or more resistant to disease through combining the genes of different species.

globalization the rapid increase in international economic, social, and technological exchange.

green revolution the change in farming methods that began in the 1940s, based on the use of chemicals and other new technologies.

growth hormones chemicals given to livestock to improve physical development.

halal meaning "lawful"; used to refer to actions such as food preparation that are permitted by Islamic law.

intensive farming a method of farming in which the maximum number of crops and livestock are grown or raised on large areas of land.

kosher conforming to Jewish religious law.

nomad a person who travels in search of food or grazing land for animals.

overfishing removing too many fish from the sea so there are not enough left to breed and renew stocks.

resource a substance that is considered valuable to humans, such as minerals, water, natural gas, or oil.

pesticides chemicals sprayed on crops to kill insects or other pests that might destroy them.

Slow Food Movement a group that supports local and organically produced food and opposes factory farming, fast food, and GM products.

staple a food that forms an essential part of diet, such as potatoes, rice, or wheat.

subsidies payments usually made by governments to support producers in a particular industry, such as agriculture.

subsistence farming a method of farming that produces just enough food for the farmer's family to eat.

surplus an amount above what is required.

toxins poisonous substances.

vitamins natural substances found in food or produced in the body by exposure to sunlight, for example, that are essential for health.

wholesale the sale of goods in large quantities to retailers, who then sell the goods to consumers at a higher price.

yield the amount of a crop that is harvested.

Index